NAVIGATING L❤VE AND IMMIGRATION

The Essential U.S. Marriage Green Card Guide for Couples

MEGAN PASTRANA

NAVIGATING LOVE AND IMMIGRATION®

The Essential U.S. Marriage Green Card Guide for Couples

For bulk orders or to request information on having Megan Pastrana appear for a speaking engagement, please contact office@immigrationforcouples.com.

Immigration for Couples®
immigrationforcouples.com

Edited by Mary Rembert
Book Design by Transcendent Publishing

ISBN: 979-8-9922207-5-9

Printed in the United States of America.

"Pressure can burst a pipe, or pressure can make a diamond."

–Robert Horry

CONTENTS

DEDICATION

To my beloved husband, Carlos, whose unwavering love and support turned our immigration journey into a beautiful adventure. Together, we inspire each other to dream bigger every day.

To my parents and grandparents, thank you for always encouraging me to reach for the stars and for helping to make my dreams of becoming an immigration attorney a reality. I am eternally grateful for your love and support.

FOREWORD

In today's polarized climate, writing a book about United States immigration is not for the faint of heart—but it's a journey filled with stories of hope, resilience, and the pursuit of a better future.

There are vast amounts of information and misinformation available online, along with anecdotes, opinions, and political rhetoric readily shared throughout society. Sifting through the noise to find clarity and confidence in moving forward can be a herculean task for someone new to the immigration world. If you can relate, I am so glad you found this book!

As with most challenging journeys, having a knowledgeable, experienced, and skillful guide along the path is not just a luxury but a necessity when navigating the labyrinth of U.S. immigration. Many guides are available in the U.S., but it's rare to find one fueled by a passion for the people involved, a deep appreciation for the nuances of the law, personal experience with the immigration process, and a desire to serve as many remarkable families seeking unification in the U.S. as possible.

It has been my privilege to work alongside Attorney Megan Pastrana, Founder and CEO of Immigration for Couples, as she has taken her lifelong dream of helping couples and families world-wide unite through the immigration process in a truly special way.

Megan has been at the forefront of ushering in a new era of legal services with her truly unique approach to serving our clients. Focusing on a holistic strategy, proactive preparation, creative advocacy, and a heart-centered approach, Megan has positioned Immigration for Couples as a leader in couples-based immigration law.

I have been involved with the firm's inner workings for some time as the Firm Administrator of Immigration for Couples. Having worked in law firms for most of my career as a paralegal and later in law firm operations, I have worked with various leadership and management styles. What surprised me most when I started working with Megan was her astounding commitment to growth. I'm not necessarily talking about the type of growth represented by dollar signs or the number of clients, but instead, the type of growth that comes with the expansion of our abilities, pushing ourselves out of our comfort zones, welcoming innovation, and more importantly, a commitment to growing as a human being.

Growth is a core value at Immigration for Couples because, without it, we can fall stagnant in how we approach our work in the world and our lives in general. As I have learned in my time here, immigration is an ever-changing beast subject to bureaucratic strongholds and political climates.

With each case our team takes on, a new set of unique circumstances and potential challenges arise, requiring our team to stretch and grow in how to best support our clients. Even cases that seem like a "slam dunk" can be thrown into limbo with one policy change, a new requirement at a local immigration office, an inconsistent decision by an official, or any number of potential delays.

As you'll learn later in the book, Megan and our team of experts have navigated almost every immigration challenge you can think of with a fair amount of fortitude and creative advocacy. I have watched Megan skillfully craft solutions to complex immigration issues that have brought our clients resolutions in months rather than the years they had been told by others to expect.

I think of Immigration for Couples as a living, breathing extension of Megan's personality—dedicated to excellence, hardworking, passionate, confident, and exuding compassion. The beauty of this mindset in a leader is that it's infectious. Our team finds true value and meaning in their work in the world. We take pride in the many ways we get to assist our clients in fulfilling their dreams.

One of our favorite sayings is "We love love" because it reflects our deep affection for the thousands of love stories we have been honored to play a part in. There's something incredibly special about knowing that what we do each day will have a meaningful impact on the lives of our clients and their love stories.

In these pages, you will find the experience and expertise that Megan has honed over her years of tireless work for her clients. She will discuss the various options that couples have when they first decide to start a life together and bravely embark on the immigration process.

You'll find education, experience, testimonials, and inspiration, and you'll receive access to some valuable resources that our team created to make your immigration experience easier. By the end of this book, we hope you have found clarity, optimism, and peace of mind to spur you forward, no matter which phase of the journey you're on.

I encourage you to find hope in the words of our former and current clients who have gone through the process. Focus on the success stories they share despite the incredibly challenging odds they were facing. Dedicate yourselves to an optimistic mindset that regularly reminds you that no matter what you and your loved one face, you will get through it and grow stronger together because of it.

Be intentional as you continue to get to know each other on a deeper level, and allow the distance to bring you closer. If you get time together, be present, make memories, and savor those moments until you can be together again. After all, this is one part of your story, but your relationship is the true journey.

–Julie Ayers, Firm Administrator, Immigration for Couples

INTRODUCTION

Embarking on the journey to obtain a U.S. marriage green card can be a mix of excitement and trepidation. For many couples, the immigration process represents not just a legal hurdle but a vital step toward building a shared future.

As an immigration attorney with years of experience guiding hundreds of couples through this complex landscape, I've seen the challenges, heartaches, and triumphs that accompany this journey.

Experiencing the immigration process firsthand with my husband has profoundly informed my understanding of these challenges, strengthening my commitment to serve as a guide and advocate for others navigating the U.S. immigration process.

My Journey Through the Process

I vividly remember the day my husband and I met. We were both attending a charity masquerade party and were seated beside one another. Mutual friends introduced us, and there was an instant connection. We began talking and then salsa dancing the night away. The next day, we went on our first date, and the rest, as they say, is history.

When we decided to get married, Carlos and I consulted several immigration attorneys. Some incorrectly told us that we did not have options, and others did not seem to care about us as human beings or as a couple. We felt as if we were just another case or transaction. Frankly, it was disheartening, but I am not one to give up easily.

I was in law school at the time, so I began doing independent research. I ultimately discovered that we had options and that a series of complex steps were involved. Not wanting to take any chances, I completed the case under the supervision of a licensed attorney, who was also my mentor in law school.

After several sets of applications, an interview, and lots of waiting, Carlos was approved for his green card. We were ecstatic to make it to the finish line. At that moment, I realized I wanted to dedicate my life to helping other couples reach their immigration goals.

That was one of those puzzle-piece moments in my life that propelled me toward my career and life's work in helping couples navigate the U.S. immigration process. To think that I almost did not attend the event that night makes me so grateful for my last-minute decision to go. That serendipitous moment was what led me to the love of my life and to embark on my own immigration journey.

I like to joke that my husband and I were my first clients. I still remember all the feelings that arose throughout the process: fear, uncertainty, overwhelm, and doubt. It was stressful, but we became more resilient as individuals and as a couple.

I love Robert Horry's quote, "Pressure can burst a pipe, or pressure can make a diamond." It is an extremely accurate description of the two paths an immigration case can take for couples. Sadly, for some couples, the pressure and stress consume them, and it leads to relationship issues or, in worst-case scenarios, breakups or divorce. However, if you are willing to receive the lessons the process can bring, the experience can be beautiful for your union.

Carlos and I have been together for over 15 years, and he is now a U.S. citizen. I look back on everything we have been through together and am so grateful for every moment of our journey.

*   *   *

Knowing how daunting the process can be, I hope this book will serve as a trusted guide, helping you navigate the intricacies of marriage-based immigration with confidence and clarity.

The following pages are designed for couples at various stages of their immigration journey. Whether you are just beginning to explore your options or are knee-deep in paperwork and waiting for important interviews, this book will provide the essential information you need to take informed action.

I've witnessed far too many couples experience "paralysis by analysis"—overwhelming confusion fueled by conflicting information and the fear of making a wrong turn. I intend to equip you with a reliable resource thoughtfully compiled to keep you from getting bogged down by the complexities of immigration law.

In Chapter 1, "The Power of Taking Swift Action," I emphasize the importance of not letting fear and uncertainty stall your progress. Countless couples have expressed their regrets over delaying the start of their immigration journey, wishing they had acted sooner despite their overwhelming emotions. It's natural to feel apprehensive when facing decisions that affect your future, especially when family and friends may have their own opinions or anecdotes to share. However, the key to overcoming the inertia of inaction is to provide yourself with the correct information and take that crucial first step.

Following the discussion of swift action, Chapter 2 introduces the concept of "Picking Your Path," where I outline the "Four Paths to Success" available to couples pursuing marriage-based green cards.

Understanding the nuances of each path—K-1 fiancé(e) visas, spouse visas, direct consular filing, and adjustment of status—will empower you to make informed choices tailored to your unique situation. Each path has specific requirements and implications, and I encourage you to reflect on which option resonates most with you and your partner.

As we dive deeper into each specific path, Chapters 3 through 6 unravel the intricacies of the K-1 fiancé(e) visa, spouse visas, direct consular filing, and adjustment of status, respectively. You will find clear, actionable insights on navigating each process, including key documentation, common pitfalls, and best practices to follow. I'll provide you with valuable tips and tricks that can significantly streamline the process, drawing from my experiences with countless couples.

Once you've successfully applied for your initial green card, Chapters 7 through 10 guide you through the post-approval phase, highlighting critical milestones such as gathering relationship evidence, preparing for the marriage interview, navigating the waiver process if needed, and understanding the removal of conditions that may follow your green card approval. The intricacies of these steps are crucial for couples to grasp, as they impact the longevity of your immigration status and provide a secure foundation for your future together.

Chapter 11, "Naturalization—The Finish Line!" celebrates the ultimate achievement many couples aspire to: U.S. citizenship. I will detail the naturalization process and its incredible benefits, including the opportunity to fully participate in the rights and responsibilities of citizenship.

The overall theme of this book is not just paperwork processing and legal jargon; it is about the unique experiences of love, growth, and resilience as couples navigate the immigration process together.

In Chapter 12, "Finding Joy in the Journey," I'll emphasize the importance of maintaining a positive mindset, even amidst the chaos of paperwork and uncertainty. Life is full of challenges, and every hurdle presents an opportunity for growth. It's essential to embrace the journey, supporting each other and celebrating the milestones along the way.

Finally, Chapter 13, "Words of Wisdom from Experienced Couples," will offer pearls of insight from those who have walked this path before you. Their stories will provide encouragement and hope, reminding you that you are not alone in this process and success is within your reach.

Through this book, I aim to foster community among couples on similar journeys. I want you to understand that every step taken together, no matter how daunting, brings you closer to a brighter future. By providing the knowledge, resources, and encouragement you need, I hope to inspire you to take swift action and navigate your immigration journey with confidence.

Your story is important, and I truly believe that love can conquer all obstacles—not only within the realm of immigration but in every aspect of life. Let's embark on this journey together, empowered with the knowledge to take decisive action toward your future. Welcome to the journey—let's begin!

CHAPTER 1

THE POWER OF TAKING SWIFT ACTION

What is the number one regret I hear from couples going through the marriage immigration process? Time and time again, the couples I meet will tell me how they wished they had started the process sooner. They tell stories of how they spent hours upon hours diving into the depths of the internet to research all the available couples-based immigration options while trying to piece all the information together to decide which path would be best for them. The sheer volume of information and misinformation available can be daunting to sift through. The overwhelm this can cause has brought many of these couples to a place I call "paralysis by analysis."

Paralysis by analysis is common when people are faced with making decisions that can impact the trajectory of their lives. There are very real consequences and challenges associated with each option that can make picking a path feel larger than life. How do you know if the information you have is accurate? Who do you trust with so much on the line? When immigration policies change, how do you navigate them? At times, it is normal to feel like you have a lot more questions than answers.

From my experience, well-meaning friends and family can also offer their opinions and anecdotes about the best way to proceed. While they are well-intended, this can add more layers of uncertainty to the mix.

Sometimes, a couple may face a decision that is upsetting for their family or that goes against their cultural norms. Immigration touches every aspect of a couple's life, and that's why there are so many dynamics at play when considering how to move forward with an immigration case.

There is nothing wrong with researching or asking for help to make an informed decision. We should all advocate for and arm ourselves with the correct information on any legal journey. The trouble can come when the fear of making the wrong decision begins to delay action. We can easily become stuck in a place of inaction because the options are many, and the consequences can be life-changing.

If I have learned anything by working in the field of immigration, it is that taking the first leap to start the process is the most important and empowered decision you can make. One of my favorite quotes comes from the great Yogi Berra, who said, "When you come to a fork in the road, take it!" I love this quote because it emphasizes that the most essential part of any decision is to make the decision.

My goal with this book is to provide a reliable resource to educate you and your significant other about what to expect during your upcoming immigration process. Hopefully, including all the fundamentals in one place will keep you from getting mired in paralysis by analysis!

I hope this book serves as a stepping stone for you to take swift action toward your future. However, individual people are different in terms of the level of detail they prefer to take in. Some readers may use this book for additional research and exploration. Other readers may be fully satisfied by what this book contains and move straight to hiring an attorney to represent them in their process. Still other readers may feel overwhelmed as soon as they open Chapter 2 and start reading about legal requirements.

There is no shame in recognizing who you are and what works best for you. I mention this ahead of time because if you notice feelings of overwhelm creeping in as you read, remember that there are other great ways to take swift action that do not require you to know the nitty-gritty technicalities.

Perhaps it would be best for you to move directly toward working with an experienced immigration lawyer who you can trust to handle things for you. Whatever you do, don't stay standing at the figurative "fork in the road"! Take swift action to move toward your best life now.

CHAPTER 2

PICK A PATH

Now that I've convinced you of the importance of taking swift action, it's time to discuss your best path forward. You may be surprised to learn that there is more than one way to apply for a marriage-based green card. In fact, there are FOUR different paths that couples commonly take! I call these the "Four Paths to Success."

There is a lot to consider when deciding which of these Four Paths is best for you. Depending on your personal circumstances, you may have only one viable option available. Or you may have two or three options and have the luxury (and challenge!) of deciding which path you prefer.

In this chapter, my goal is to provide an overview of the Four Paths to help you better understand your options as you decide which path to embark on with your partner. I'll give you a brief summary of each path now. You can mentally note which path or paths sound most promising and then read the corresponding chapters that follow, which describe each path in finer detail.

Remember that there is no one "best" option that everyone prefers. Each path has unique benefits, limitations, legal requirements, and eligibility factors. But most importantly, each path—when followed correctly with the assistance of an experienced immigration attorney—leads to a successful outcome in the form of a green card. This status, which in formal legal terms is called "lawful permanent residence," will allow a foreign citizen to live and work indefinitely in the United States as long as they follow certain maintenance requirements. Lawful permanent residence is also the foundation of the potential opportunity to become a U.S. citizen for residents who choose to do so.

The Four Paths to Success

K-1 Fiancé(e) Visa

A fiancé(e) visa is designed to bring an unmarried foreign partner of a U.S. citizen to the U.S. for 90 days so that they can get married. After the marriage, the foreign spouse remains in the U.S. while the couple applies for a green card based on the marriage.

If you and your partner have already completed a legal marriage anywhere in the world, the K-1 fiancé(e) visa is NOT for you; you will instead need to pick one of the other three paths for couples who are already legal spouses.

Likewise, if having your wedding outside the U.S. or waiting inside the U.S. for the green card to process is a deal-breaker for you, then the K-1 is not the right choice.

Spouse Visa

A spouse visa is the legal default option for married couples. It is designed to bring a foreign spouse of a U.S. citizen or green card

holder from abroad to the United States, although it is also sometimes used for foreign nationals who are already in the U.S.

If you are married and eligible for only one option, it will be this
one! That makes the spouse visa a great place to start with your
research and understanding of the immigration process.

The spouse visa application process culminates at a U.S. Embassy
in a foreign country where the visa is issued. Once the visa is used
to enter the U.S. within the specified time period, the foreign citizen automatically becomes a permanent resident, with no additional applications required inside the United States.

Direct Consular Filing

A direct consular filing is a variation of the standard spouse visa
process. It is only available when the petitioning U.S. spouse lives
abroad with the foreign spouse. This process has many restrictions, and it is not possible in all countries. However, for couples
who qualify, a direct consular filing can cut several months or
even years off the overall processing time!

Adjustment of Status

Adjustment of status is a legal process done at an office inside the
United States. It is for foreign nationals already inside the U.S. (such
as on a student visa or temporary work visa) who want to become
lawful permanent residents based on their marriage. Spouses of
both U.S. citizens and green card holders can adjust their status,
but the rules are significantly more complicated and restrictive for
the spouses of green card holders to adjust their status.

Adjustment of status in most cases requires the foreign spouse to
stay in the United States for a period of time during the processing,

which some couples don't mind. However, some couples will decide to forego adjustment of status and do a spouse visa instead if frequent international travel is important to the foreign spouse.

Now that you know a bit about each of the Four Paths to Success, you may be especially curious to explore one or two of these options in more detail. The next four chapters explore each of the Four Paths in greater detail. I have written them so that you don't need to read them in chronological order. (Although the direct consular filing chapter will probably make more sense if you read the chapter on general spouse visas first.)

So dig in however you wish! Here are the corresponding chapter topics so you can flip ahead:

Chapter 3: K-1 Fiancé(e) Visas

Chapter 4: Spouse Visas

Chapter 5: Direct Consular Filing

Chapter 6: Adjustment of Status

After that, we will continue to cover the milestones of your immigration journey that happen after you have used one of the Four Paths to get your initial green card!

As you embark on your journey to choose the best path for your marriage-based green card application, I invite you to download our free comprehensive guide, which offers an overview of the four processes, including eligibility requirements and the pros and cons of each option—all presented in an easy-to-read chart format. Visit **immigrationforcouples.com/book-vip** to access your free guide and take the first step toward a successful immigration journey together!

CHAPTER 3

K-1 FIANCÉ(E) VISAS

One popular path to a green card is a K-1 fiancé(e) visa. If you and your partner are not yet legally married, this option is worth considering. (And if you are already married, no worries! Move to the next chapter because this doesn't apply to you.)

Fiancé(e) visas have become more prominent in pop culture in recent years, thanks to highly entertaining reality TV shows on the topic, like *90 Day Fiancé* and related spinoffs. Although I love to watch the drama go down on those episodes as much as you do, I've noticed that the shows tend to gloss over the legal nuances of how couples actually get and use their visas.

So, how do you know if a K-1 fiancé(e) visa is right for you? Where would you start if you decided on this path? Let's talk through what to expect!

What benefit does a K-1 visa provide?

The foreign fiancé(e) of a U.S. citizen can use a K-1 visa to enter the U.S. once and lawfully stay for up to 90 days. Then, they must either get married or depart the country. If they get married, the immigrant spouse can remain in the country while completing the green card application process.

Who is eligible for a K-1 fiancé(e) visa?

There are a few requirements that you will have to meet to be able to get a K-1 fiancé(e) visa:

- **The petitioning partner must be a U.S. citizen.** It is NOT enough to be a lawful permanent resident with a green card. If the petitioner is only a resident, they can either go through the naturalization process to become a U.S. citizen before beginning the K-1 process, or the couple can choose another immigration option, such as a spouse visa.

- **You intend to get married within the 90-day visa period.** One of the ways that the U.S. government confirms whether this is true for you or not is by asking for evidence that you have established a close relationship and that you're nearly ready for marriage. However, keep in mind that it is okay if you are not already 100% ready to marry. Some couples know they need more time together before they are completely ready for the ceremony. The foreign fiancé(e) may want to get a feel for life in the U.S. and settle in before making things official. As long as you intend to marry (or make a final marriage decision) within those 90 days of the visa validity, you are using the visa as intended.

- **You are both legally free to marry.** This means that before starting the process, both of you must be legally single and able to marry each other. If you have previous marriages, the divorce or annulment must be complete before filing your application.

- **The foreign fiancé(e) is "admissible."** The U.S. immigration laws have a long list of problems that can prevent an immigrant from being allowed to get a visa or green card. These problems are called "grounds of inadmissibility." Someone who does not have any of these problems is referred to as "admissible." See Chapter 9 for more information about admissibility and overcoming issues with admissibility.

- **You met each other in person at least once in the two years before filing your fiancé(e) visa petition.** This requirement comes as a surprise to some couples. Rare exceptions can qualify for a waiver of the in-person meeting requirement. To get a waiver, you would either need to show that meeting each other in person would "violate strict and long-established customs" of your culture or that having to meet in person would cause "extreme hardship" to the U.S. citizen fiancé(e).

Why do we have to meet in person? What if we haven't met yet?

You may be wondering why immigration would have a strict requirement like this because it would seem that if a couple is in love but may not have the means to meet up as often, they should not be penalized, right?

Immigration has this requirement and others to prevent immigration fraud, which can occur when people try to obtain entry into the U.S. by cutting corners or not really being a couple. Most of the eligibility requirements were put in place to deter people from faking a relationship to gain a green card in the U.S.

In this modern online dating world, meeting someone at least once in person can help prevent Americans from being targets of catfishing-style dating scams. It's sad but true that this is the world we live in!

How can we prepare to apply for a K-1 fiancé(e) visa?

If you've decided that the K-1 fiancé(e) visa is going to be the best option for you and your significant other, then there are some preliminary things you can start doing right away to get yourselves in a good position to start.

- **Collect personal data:** The application forms to start the multiphase K-1 application process involve many specific details about each partner's life and personal history. Many of my clients over the years have mentioned that they found the most onerous task to be gathering the last five years' worth of their employment histories and places of residence. Gathering this information ahead of time can help things go more smoothly.

- **Collect required documents:** There are several required documents for your application packet. This list changes periodically, but some documents are always there—like valid, unexpired identification documents and birth certificates. You also should save any documents that prove you've met in person in the last two years. The lawyer you work with for your process should give you an up-to-date, complete list of everything you need and help determine whether you have the right things.

- **Gather relationship evidence:** Another major category of documents you will need for the application is proof of your relationship. So keep all those photos, letters, message or call logs, travel documents, and anything else that shows you are truly a couple in love!

Once you have gathered all the needed information and documents, your legal team can begin drafting the application packet.

What happens when we file the petition?

The petition application packet filing is the first step in the K-1 fiancé(e) visa process. It is filed on paper or electronically with U.S. Citizenship and Immigration Services (USCIS). Shortly after filing, you will receive a paper I-797 "Notice of Action" in the mail from USCIS confirming your application was received and entered into the system. It will also let you know the case number assigned to your case and which processing center is working on your file. These details are important for future tracking and follow-up purposes!

Once our petition is approved, what is the next step?

This is great news, but you're not done with the process quite yet! Once the petition is approved, you must wait for your case to be transferred to the National Visa Center (NVC) and then forwarded to the U.S. Embassy.

At this step, ownership of your file transfers from the U.S. Department of Homeland Security to the U.S. Department of State, so you will no longer be inquiring with USCIS about your case status or processing time.

This part of the process involves another form called a DS160 and submitting more documents proving your identity, relationship, and the financial ability of the fiancé(e) to survive in the U.S. while on the K-1 fiancé(e) visa. You will also add any applications for children who you want to bring with you and pay visa fees.

What happens at the U.S. Embassy interview?

Once you have submitted all of the preliminary documents, your case will be cleared for scheduling an interview at your local U.S. Embassy. Depending on the country, you may also schedule appointments for your medical exam and fingerprinting for background checks.

Then, the foreign national fiancé(e) will attend an in-person interview where a U.S. consular officer will ask questions to confirm your eligibility for the K-1 fiancé(e) visa.

If all goes well, they will keep your passport and print the visa in your passport. If anything is missing from your application, you must submit additional documents or information until the consulate decides you can get the visa.

So then can I travel to the United States?

Yes, as soon as you have the K-1 fiancé(e) visa in hand, you can book your travel. Be sure to check that your name and birth date printed on the visa are correct because mistakes do happen occasionally which would need to be corrected before you travel. The visa will also have a printed expiration date, so you know you must travel to the U.S. before it expires. Usually, you will have around a 90- to 180-day window to travel, but it can vary depending on what the Embassy chooses to do, so check what is printed on your visa to be sure.

Finally, the Step You've All Been Waiting For …

Reuniting in the United States to start your lives together is the step you've been dreaming of since starting this process! Your fiancé(e) will finally be with you in the United States, and you can spend quality time together, adjust to living together, and start the wedding ceremony planning process. Yay, congratulations!

Many couples have questions about how to go about planning a wedding with such a short turnaround time. After all, in the U.S., it's not uncommon for American couples to spend one or two years planning their weddings! However, with a bit of ingenuity, you can still have a meaningful and memorable ceremony in much less time. I've had the benefit of seeing how many K-1 couples tackled the wedding planning logistics over the years, so here are my top tips to pass on to you:

Speedy Wedding Planning Tips

- **Use a flexible venue.** Rather than booking out a large venue that gets scheduled years in advance, do you have a family member or friend with a nice house or backyard you could use? Or could you use a public location informally for you and just a handful of guests?

- **Consider decorations that store well.** Thousands of dollars of high-end floral arrangements take a lot of preplanning to pull off. If there is a way to use nonfloral decorations like candles, silk flowers, or other items, you can obtain them ahead of time and store them until your wedding day. If you want fresh flowers, you could use ones that are available daily from local florists or even Costco. It is surprising what you can typically access in a pinch if you aren't set on one specific flower type!

- **Identify a few vendors to be on "standby."** Some couples screen vendors like photographers and let them know ahead of time that, due to the immigration process, it is not possible to solidify the date more than a couple of months in advance. However, you could have a short list of vendors to call once you get the visa and the date can be determined.

- **Consider less common days and times.** The most common dates to marry in your area might be Saturdays. You could consider doing an evening ceremony on another day of the week to maximize the chances that vendors and locations will be available on shorter notice.

- **Host the legal ceremony separately.** Technically, you only need to complete the legally binding portion of your wedding ceremony to file your green card application. Some couples will do a basic courthouse ceremony as soon as possible to get legally married, then plan their big party and/or religious ceremony to happen at their leisure later.

Whatever plans you make for your wedding ceremony, ensure you and your fiancé(e) feel comfortable with it. You've come so far in your journey and deserve a nice day to celebrate your love and momentarily forget about immigration paperwork!

Getting Right Back to That Paperwork

When you have your certified marriage certificate in hand, it's finally time to apply for your green card! This application is filed with USCIS and is called "adjustment of status." You can read more about the adjustment of status process in Chapter 6.

The process is very similar for couples with a K-1 fiancé(e) visa and those who are only doing an adjustment of status. However, because you already filed a petition as part of the K-1 application, in most cases, you can skip having to do another spouse petition and solely apply for the green card.

There is typically some significant wait time while the green card application is pending. Your attorney will talk to you about applying for a temporary work authorization permit and international travel authorization so that you can live more freely while the case is processing. The timeframe for processing varies depending on your location in the United States and what is happening with immigration during different eras and moments in U.S. politics.

Even in the best of circumstances, you can expect that the foreign spouse will initially have to remain in the United States for at least a few months and be unable to work lawfully until the temporary authorizations come in, so it's important to be aware of that limitation and plan accordingly.

Some Final Thoughts on the K-1 Fiancé(e) Visa Option

Overall, the K-1 fiancé(e) visa can be a great option for couples who are currently unmarried and want their foreign fiancé(e) to move to the United States as soon as possible.

Now you have a good idea of what the K-1 fiancé(e) visa process entails. Keep in mind that this is NOT the only path to a green card through marriage, though!

Keep reading to check out other common methods you can use to apply.

To further simplify your K-1 fiancé(e) visa journey, download our free comprehensive chart that breaks down the process step by step. This helpful resource provides a clear overview of each stage, ensuring you have all the information you need at your fingertips. Visit **immigrationforcouples.com/book-vip** to access your free downloadable chart and take the next step toward a successful application!

CHAPTER 4

SPOUSE VISAS

Ironically, the spouse visa is represented the least often in popular media and romcoms, but it is the most common option used by couples worldwide. As an attorney, I consider the spouse visa to be the first basic option I consider for couples who are consulting with me. Unless there is a good reason for you to select one of the other options, the spouse visa is typically the way we will go.

What benefit does a spouse visa provide?

A spouse visa is a visa printed in the foreign spouse's passport that allows them to move to the United States permanently, where they can legally work if they wish and live with their spouse. Unlike a fiancé(e) visa, a spouse visa can be used for multiple entries. Some spouses may even arrive one day on the spouse visa and then travel internationally the next day. Likewise, the foreign spouse can begin working immediately in the United States upon arrival.

Who is eligible for a spouse visa?

Of all of the marriage-based immigration pathways, spouse visas have the fewest legal requirements. For that reason, this is the pathway that we consider to be the standard option. If you qualify for anything, it will be a spouse visa. However, not every couple qualifies. Here are the most important requirements that you will have to meet to be able to get a spouse visa:

- **The petitioning partner must be a U.S. citizen or lawful permanent resident.** Unlike with fiancé(e) visas, the petitioner does not need to be a U.S. citizen to be eligible; having a green card in good standing is enough. However, the wait times for spouses of U.S. citizens are sometimes faster than for spouses of green card holders.

- **You are legally married to each other.** You must be in a legally binding marriage under the laws of either the United States or a foreign country, and you cannot have any legal flaws in your marriage. For example, prior marriages must all have been terminated through divorce, annulment, or the passing away of your previous spouse. If you were married abroad, your attorney must check the U.S. Department of State standards for accepting a marriage from that particular country, or you may run into problems as the case progresses. You also cannot begin filing your spouse visa case before the legal wedding takes place or file based on a purely religious wedding ceremony unless it occurred in a country where religious ceremonies are also recognized by the government.

- **The foreign spouse is "admissible."** The U.S. immigration laws have a long list of problems that can prevent an immigrant from being allowed to get a visa or green card. These problems are called "grounds of inadmissibility." Someone who does not have any of these problems is referred to as "admissible." See Chapter 9 for more information about admissibility and overcoming issues with admissibility.

The Spouse Visa Application Process

The spouse visa application process involves three main phases, each with several steps and different federal agencies.

Phase 1: Marriage Petition

The first step in obtaining a spouse visa is to submit an I-130 marriage petition to USCIS. In this step, the couple proves that they have a legally binding marriage and that their relationship is real.

They also prove the petitioner's immigration status as a U.S. citizen or a green card holder. Once USCIS is convinced that the marriage is legitimate and legally binding, it will approve the petition and forward the application to the National Visa Center.

Phase 2: National Visa Center

The second main phase in the spouse visa case is processing with the National Visa Center (NVC). Many different types of information and documents are submitted to the NVC.

Couples must show copies of all the personal documents they will present later at the U.S. Embassy interview, such as birth certificates, marriage documentation, and police certificates from foreign countries where they have resided.

They also must prove that they will have the necessary financial support after arrival in the United States by showing that the petitioner or a joint sponsor has the means to support the foreign spouse. In addition, the NVC collects a lot of other data about your history and background.

Once the NVC has everything it needs from you, you will be notified that you are officially being put into the queue for an interview to be scheduled at the U.S. Embassy in the country where you will be processed.

The wait time for an interview varies quite a bit depending on the country in which you are processing (usually your country of citizenship or permanent residence) and how many other people are currently waiting for interviews.

Phase 3: Consular Interview

The third phase occurs when you are scheduled for an interview at the U.S. Consulate where you are processing your case. Before attending the interview, you need to get a medical exam from a physician approved to do immigration medical exams.

The medical exam process will check to see if you have any contagious diseases of public health concern to the United States and, if you do, make sure you get treatment before a visa is issued. You may also be required to get additional vaccinations to be able to enter the United States.

The U.S. Consulate will also take your fingerprints to run a background check in some countries. There are additional countries whose specific procedures are required as well. You must also bring updated copies of your information to attend an in-person interview at the consulate.

In nearly all cases, only the foreign spouse attends the interview. Once the consulate has everything needed, they will print the spouse visa into the foreign spouse's passport.

The visa has a valid date by which they must use it for the first time to enter the United States. Once the foreign spouse uses that visa for the first time and passes through U.S. Customs, certain paperwork is filled out by the customs officer to complete the green card process. The green card is later printed by USCIS and mailed to you at your home address in the United States. Unlike with a fiancé(e) visa, there is no additional paperwork to do after arrival in the United States. You are already considered a lawful permanent resident from day one!

Why do couples choose the spouse visa option?

There are a handful of reasons why I most commonly see couples decide to take the spouse visa pathway. First, some couples may simply have the spouse visa as their only option. After all, if they are already married, they cannot apply for a fiancé(e) visa, and if the foreign spouse is abroad, they cannot apply for an adjustment of status (which I cover in more detail in Chapter 6).

However, some couples with multiple options still decide that a spouse visa is ideal. A spouse visa has the advantage of requiring less overall paperwork than a fiancé(e) visa. Spouse visas also cost less in government filing and attorney fees because fewer steps are involved.

Additionally, with a spouse visa, the foreign spouse does not have any periods in which they are "stuck" waiting in the U.S. without work authorization or the ability to travel abroad. The day they enter the United States, they can work and travel freely. For couples in which the foreign spouse does not want to have an interruption to their career or needs to be able to travel abroad at a moment's notice, the spouse visa can be an ideal option to facilitate these preferences.

A Final Word on Spouse Visas

You may already think a spouse visa is the perfect option for you. Great! Even so, read on to Chapter 5, which covers a little-known but significant variant of spouse visas available only to certain couples. I will also cover the fourth of the Four Paths to Success in Chapter 6 on the adjustment of status application.

To further simplify your spouse visa journey, download our free comprehensive chart that breaks down the process step by step. This helpful resource provides a clear overview of each stage, ensuring you have all the information you need. Visit **immigrationforcouples.com/book-vip** to access your free downloadable chart and take the next step toward a successful application!

CHAPTER 5

DIRECT CONSULAR FILING

In Chapter 4, we discussed the usual application process for obtaining a spouse visa. In this chapter, we will talk about one important variation sometimes used to obtain a spouse visa in a slightly different, but typically much faster, way. And who doesn't want their case to go faster?!

How Direct Consular Filing Is Different

The usual process that all applicants undertake to obtain their spouse visas is:

1. They send an I-130 Petition application to USCIS.

2. Once USCIS approves the petition, the file gets sent to NVC, an intermediary office that is part of the U.S. Department of State. The Department of State is also responsible for running all U.S. Embassies in foreign countries. One of the functions of the U.S. Embassies is to assess visa applicants for eligibility and, if the visa is approved, to print the visas. The NVC collects additional

information about the applicant and their spouse to confirm that the couple has all documentation ready for the Embassy to decide on the case.

3. The case gets placed on a waiting list for an available interview slot at the appropriate Embassy. Once an interview appointment is assigned, the applicant undergoes a medical exam and a security background check and attends the interview. At this interview, a consular officer makes a final decision on the visa application.

As you can imagine from this very brief summary of everything that happens in a typical spouse visa case, going through all of these steps with three different entities (two of which are in different federal agencies) takes a lot of time.

Direct consular filing is different because all these same steps are compressed into one step that is handled in its entirety by the U.S. Embassy. The I-130 Petition, all the documents that would have gone to the NVC, and everything related to the interview are reviewed onsite, and if all is good, the visa is issued.

If that sounds incredibly awesome to you, I completely agree! It is always wonderful when we can get everything taken care of swiftly through direct consular filing.

The only reason direct consular filing is not awesome is that very few couples meet the requirements and are permitted to direct consular file.

So, let's talk now about those restrictions and requirements.

Who Is Eligible for Direct Consular Filing?

A petitioner must live abroad with a spouse. To even consider a direct consular filing, you have to be in a situation where the U.S. and foreign spouse are already living together abroad. If you aren't, you should do the regular spouse visa process or one of the other options instead.

Couples must live in a country where this service is available. It would be logical to assume that since the U.S. Department of State manages the operations of all U.S. Embassies, all the U.S. Embassies would run the same way.

Interestingly enough, this could not be further from the truth. There are numerous quirks and differences between the various embassies, and understanding the methods and preferences of each one is an important part of how my team represents clients.

However, for purposes of direct consular filing, there are only some countries where it is possible to direct consular file, and the countries where it is possible vary over time. For clients who could be eligible for direct consular filing, I research to determine whether their local embassy has been authorized to accept direct consular filings, and if so, whether or not they are actually accepting these filings and what their preferred process is.

Couples must meet any country-specific requirements. In addition to being authorized to accept direct consular filings, an embassy may have additional restrictions or limitations on which types of cases they will accept.

For example, as of this book's publication date, most embassies accepting direct filings require showing some type of emergency humanitarian situation or proof that the U.S. spouse would be relocating to the U.S. for a job with little advance notice. A couple living abroad may not be approved to direct consular file their case.

Embassy personnel is responsive. Because direct consular filing is relatively rare and restricted, many countries where it is accepted do not have a clear process for initiating a direct consular file.

Over the years, I have learned a lot about the best ways to get the attention of consular personnel and what to say to maximize my client's chances of being accepted to direct consular file. However, sometimes, even with my best efforts and know-how, the consular post simply does not respond. When this is the case, we must move forward with a standard spouse visa application process.

A petitioner must be eligible for a spouse visa. Maybe it goes without saying, but I did want to make it clear that all of the other requirements for spouse visas also apply in this case. Direct consular filing is a way to make the process go faster, but it does not in any way circumvent any of the other legal requirements.

Can I try both methods of filing a spouse visa simultaneously?

In a word, no. Once a petition has been filed with USCIS, it is virtually impossible to get an embassy to entertain the possibility of accepting a direct consular file. That's one of the reasons it is so important to have good legal advice for your case before sending in a single document!

I have seen numerous couples over the years attempt to begin their immigration cases without assistance and then realize that they need help. By the time they come to see me, it's not always possible for me to undo all the missteps they have already made, such as rendering themselves ineligible for direct consular filing by starting their case in another way.

Do I have to direct consular file if I'm eligible?

No, you could simply do the normal spouse visa application process even if the petitioner lives abroad. Direct consular filing is a voluntary, possible optional process that some couples find advantageous, but no one has to use it under any circumstances.

CHAPTER 6

ADJUSTMENT OF STATUS

The first three Paths to Success we covered in this book involved methods to bring a foreign partner outside of the United States into the United States by obtaining a visa.

However, some foreign nationals are already in the United States when they begin the marriage-based immigration process to apply for a green card. For most of these already in-country immigrants, adjusting status is the best method to select.

What benefit does adjustment of status provide?

Adjustment of status is beneficial because it allows foreign spouses already in the United States to remain in the country with their spouses while applying for their green cards. For those who already live in the United States, adjustment of status causes less hassle, expense, and frustration than having to travel internationally to complete the visa process at a U.S. Embassy abroad.

Another benefit of adjustment of status is that it's the only path that allows the immigrant to obtain temporary work authorization while the case is pending.

Who is eligible to adjust status?

- **The petitioning partner must be a U.S. citizen or lawful permanent resident.** Unlike fiancé(e) visas, the petitioner does not need to be a U.S. citizen to be eligible; having a green card in good standing is enough. However, although some green card holders can sponsor their spouses for an adjustment of status, there are certain benefits for U.S. citizens who are applying for adjustment of status of their spouses that cause some couples to wait until the petitioner becomes a U.S. citizen before filing adjustment of status.

  * Heads Up!* If the petitioner has a green card, you should consult an experienced immigration lawyer before filing an adjustment of status based on your marriage because your eligibility depends on several variables, including the current status of annual immigrant visa caps, USCIS filing rules for the month, and whether or not the beneficiary has ever been out of lawful status or violated the conditions of their status in the U.S.

- **You must be in a legally binding marriage under the laws of either the United States or a foreign country, and you cannot have any legal flaws in your marriage.** For example, prior marriages must all have been terminated through divorce, annulment, or the passing away of your previous spouse.

- **The foreign spouse must be "admissible."** The U.S. immigration laws have a long list of problems that can prevent an immigrant from being allowed to get a visa or green card. These problems are called "grounds of inadmissibility." Someone who does not have any of these problems is referred to as "admissible." See Chapter 9 for more information about admissibility and overcoming problems with admissibility.

- **The foreign spouse has to be physically inside the U.S. when filing.** If they are living abroad or are currently abroad, even temporarily, for any reason, you cannot file an adjustment of status. There are also strict rules that, in many cases, require the foreign spouse to stay in the United States continuously while the case is pending (more about that later in this chapter).

- **The foreign spouse's most recent entry to the U.S. was lawful.** It is not enough for the beneficiary spouse to be in the United States at the moment. The laws for adjustment of status say that they had to have entered legally, or as we say in legal terms, "lawfully admitted or paroled." In plain language, the foreign spouse came in with a visa, the Visa Waiver Program (using ESTA), or otherwise spoke with a U.S. customs officer at an airport or the border and was allowed to enter the country. Rare exceptions to this rule allow some people who did not enter lawfully to still adjust status. Consulting an experienced immigration lawyer will help you determine whether any exceptions apply to you or if you need to apply for a spouse visa instead.

What is the application process for an adjustment of status case?

Unlike the other paths we have previously discussed, adjustment of status allows all necessary paperwork to be filed in a single step with USCIS. Most clients send their petition, green card application, and requests for temporary work and travel authorization altogether, along with all other required forms and evidence.

Once the application is received by USCIS, they send you a receipt notice as proof of acceptance. The receipt notice also has a case number assignment, so it is easier to track the progress of your case through the system.

Next, you will receive a notice for a biometrics appointment. This quick appointment is designed solely to take your photo, fingerprints, and identifying information like hair and eye color to run background checks on you.

Normally, at least three months into the processing time of the case (and sometimes significantly longer than that), you will receive the temporary work authorization and temporary international travel authorization. This is intended to make life easier for you while waiting to receive your green card.

At some point later in the waiting, you will receive a notice for an interview appointment. This is the more intensive appointment where you and your spouse will be personally interviewed by an officer about your relationship and eligibility. (See Chapter 8 for more details on marriage interviews.)

Once your case is approved, the green card will be printed and mailed to your house. You are now a lawful permanent resident!

What if I'm not in the U.S., but I'd like to adjust status?

Adjustment of status is only an option for foreign nationals who are already inside the U.S. for another purpose. Some individuals try to use tourist visas or other strategies to get into the U.S. to adjust, but this is risky, and I don't recommend it. There are strict rules in the immigration laws that limit your options and ability to adjust status if you have entered the U.S. on a different temporary visa type with the intention to stay and adjust your status.

This is a very different situation than an immigrant who enters the U.S. for the stated purpose of their visa (for example, to start an MBA program) and their circumstances change after they are already here (for example, they meet the love of their life in class after starting their program, get married, and decide to stay). This area of the law is complex; I recommend you get legal advice about your eligibility for adjustment of status.

Do I need to stay in the U.S. the whole time while my adjustment of status is pending?

Generally, yes. The immigration laws say that if you leave the U.S. while your adjustment of status is pending, it is considered to be legally abandoning your case, and the case will automatically be denied. If you need to depart the U.S., you can apply for a travel authorization to allow you to leave while your case is pending.

However, there are a few exceptions, such as some individuals on H1B visas, for example. This is due to a specific feature of the legal basis of this visa type, which makes it an exception to the abandonment rule for adjustment of status.

Can I lawfully work while my case is pending?

Some individuals can legally work in the U.S. while their adjustment of status is pending, and others cannot, or cannot for part of the application processing time. You should speak with an immigration attorney about your specific circumstances to see whether you can continue working on the current visa you hold. Most adjustment of status applicants apply for temporary work authorization along with their adjustment application so that they can work for at least part of the time the case is processing.

To further simplify your adjustment of status journey, download our free comprehensive chart that breaks down the process step by step. This helpful resource provides a clear overview of each stage, ensuring you have all the information you need. Visit **immigrationforcouples.com/book-vip** to access your free downloadable chart and take the next step toward a successful application!

CHAPTER 7

RELATIONSHIP EVIDENCE

We've discussed the Four Paths to Success, but now we are moving on to an important topic common to all of the paths: how to prove to the U.S. government that your relationship is legitimate. This is a critical requirement for every single type of marriage-based immigration case. All government officers making case-related decisions want to verify whether your relationship is "bona fide."

How does the government know if your relationship is bona fide?

So, how does the government know if a relationship is legitimate? Realistically, they can't look inside your mind and heart to discover your secret intentions. Instead, government officials depend on a process that examines the circumstantial evidence about your intentions. They ask for documentary evidence to be filed with the paperwork. A trained interviewer assesses your demeanor and testimony given in a live interview. They Google you and check out your social media. (Come on, you would do it too if you had their job! Social media made this process a lot easier for them.) They also have a fraud team that performs other types of traditional detective work, if necessary, such as investigating the accuracy of the documents you provided and what you said during your interview.

Wait, they have fraud investigators?

Many of our clients are surprised to learn that this is true. However, the fraud team is not involved in all cases (as far as the public currently knows). The government officers at U.S. Citizenship and Immigration Services can flag cases that seem suspicious and refer them to the fraud team for further investigation. Fraud investigators have been known to show up randomly and talk with neighbors and family members of the immigrant and the United States citizen spouse, as well as to confirm details of bank statements and lease documentation submitted with an application.

In recent years, fraud investigators have even been on the ground in foreign countries, investigating things such as the legitimacy of court records supposedly issued by foreign judges.

As they say, "The best defense is a good offense." That's why it's important to have solid documentation of your relationship to submit with your case. My goal with my clients is always for the government officer to take one look at their well-supported case and think, "This looks legit," and stamp them through to the next step in the process without needing to investigate further.

Types of Evidence the Government Looks For

There are a few categories of evidence that historically USCIS and the U.S. Department of State have found to be the most convincing in proving that a relationship is bona fide. This includes things like:

- Proof that you live together
- Proof that you have joined your finances together
- Proof that you are in regular communication with each other
- Proof that your relationship is publicly known (not a secret)
- Proof that you spend time together and make joint decisions

Obviously, not all of these categories apply to every single couple. For example, your spouse may be living abroad until they receive their spouse visa, so you may need to rely more heavily on other evidence since you don't live together yet.

Examples of Classic Relationship Evidence

Now that you understand what main categories are most helpful to prove, I'd like to give you some specific examples of types of documents that you may have that could help you prove these categories. Keep in mind that these are simply some examples of commonly used documents. Every couple is different, and when I represent them, I help them make a customized strategy for the most convincing evidence to use in their specific situation.

However, it can be helpful to understand ahead of time what types of documents are commonly used so that you can begin saving items that could potentially be useful evidence for your case.

Proof You Live Together (or Visit Each Other)

- Current joint apartment lease

- Past joint apartment leases
- Deed to home
- Mortgage statement in both names
- Household bills in both of your names together
- Household bills in your separate names but showing the same address
- Plane tickets, car rentals, hotel receipts, or toll road payments from visits back and forth to each other
- Copy of passport stamps or visas showing you've visited each other's countries

Proof of Kids or Pets (if Applicable)

- Birth certificates of any children you have together
- Pet adoption records
- Photos of you with kids and/or pets

Proof of Ongoing Communication

- Printouts of text messages by phone
- Cell phone call logs or bills showing regular calls
- Screenshots of you video-chatting together
- WhatsApp or Facebook Messenger printouts

Proof of Joint Finances

- Bank statements from joint accounts
- Statements from shared credit card accounts

- Insurance documents with both names (health, dental, vision, home, auto)
- Life insurance policy listing spouse as beneficiary
- Joint car title
- Loan documents if you've ever borrowed money together or co-signed a loan

Testimonials From People You Know

- Notarized letters from friends and family describing your relationship. They should include their contact information and describe specific instances when they have seen you interact.

The "Mushy" Stuff

- Love letters or cards to and from each other
- Photos together. Try to select photos that show time passing (you have different hairstyles, different seasons or holidays, or look younger, etc.), show you with friends and family, show you celebrating holidays or important events, and show the wedding and reception or engagement parties, etc.
- Wedding-related evidence such as ring purchases, vendors' receipts, etc.

Hopefully, this list will give you a better idea of the documents that can be useful as evidence that your relationship is bona fide!

CHAPTER 8

THE MARRIAGE INTERVIEW

It's the stuff old-school romantic comedies are made of: an anxious couple separated at the immigration office is grilled by a serious-looking officer about the details of their personal life. Will she forget the color of his toothbrush? Will he flub the middle name of her great aunt, who lives five states over? Tensions are high, but somehow you just know these two lovebirds will live happily ever after in fairytale style …

Like most topics, Hollywood's take on the marriage interview process is based on a grain of truth but then stretched beyond recognition for dramatic effect. In this chapter, we'll discuss the reality of who undergoes marriage immigration interviews and what these interviews are actually like.

Although I definitely hope you have a fairytale ending in your relationship and immigration case, my goal is to see you get there without any tense moments of government interrogation like the protagonists of your favorite movies.

Which couples have a marriage interview as part of their process?

Some of my clients have been completely shocked to find out that, unlike in the movies, not all couples even have a marriage green card interview as part of their immigration application process. If you are applying for a spouse visa, the only interview that will take place is the foreign national spouse who is interviewed individually at a U.S. Embassy as part of their process. It is rare that a U.S. Embassy would even allow, much less request, the presence of the petitioner's spouse at one of these interviews, so if you are going the traditional spouse visa route, you can say goodbye to your anticipated Hollywood moment!

Fiancé(e) visa applicants are also interviewed at the U.S. Embassy. However, after they come to the United States and marry, they are usually still interviewed as a couple as part of their adjustment of status process. So, if you plan on taking the fiancé(e) visa path, you typically will be interviewed during the latter part of your immigration journey.

The same thing goes for the adjustment of status applicants. They are almost always personally interviewed as a couple by a USCIS officer at a USCIS field office somewhere in the United States. Most traditional stereotypes or representations of a marriage-based interview are mimicking, although exaggerating, the adjustment of status application process.

However, some couples with an adjustment of status case have their interviews waived. Although it is legally possible for the government to waive interviews for couples, whether or not they are doing so at any given moment tends to be a function of politics and current policies.

Don't read too much into whether your interview is waived or not. Couples sometimes wonder if it's a bad sign that they're scheduled for an interview because they are worried that the government may find their case suspicious. This is definitely not true, as most couples who complete the adjustment of status process are interviewed in person regardless of the strength of their application.

What happens at the interview?

You will attend the interview with your spouse at the scheduled date and time sent to you by USCIS. There is a check-in process, and then you wait in the waiting room as if you were going to a doctor's appointment or something similar.

At some point, an officer will come out and call your names and take you to the back, where they have individual offices set up for interviewing applicants. In some offices, it's more common to separate couples and interview only one spouse at a time. In other USCIS offices, couples are typically interviewed together for an initial interview.

In some areas, additional subsequent types of interviews can occur, sometimes referred to as "Stokes interviews," where the couple is always separated, and the interview is more intense due to a suspicion of fraud.

In recent years, we have seen that USCIS relies more on a team of on-the-ground investigators to check the veracity of the evidence and the couple's relationship that they have identified as potentially having fraudulent relationships rather than calling these couples in for additional interviews to make a final determination.

For the interview, both spouses will raise their right hands and swear under penalty of perjury that everything they say in the interview is true. The interviews are typically videotaped. The officer will then review all the filed forms for accuracy and make any needed corrections or updates. Then, they will spend some time asking about topics related to your relationship.

Questions Usually Asked at the Interview

We tend to see officers cover a few topic areas in their questioning. Keep in mind that it is more of a two-way conversation with the officer than them grilling you on facts and figures and stats about your spouse. Typically, they will start with questions in one of these categories, and then, depending on your answers, they will ask further detailed questions to follow up.

For example, if they ask if you've taken any trips lately and you respond that you took a weekend getaway to a nearby city, they will ask in more detail exactly what you did on your trip together.

I've represented clients in hundreds of marriage interviews at USCIS offices across the country, and these are the main topics I have seen officers ask about:

Relationship History

Officers like to ask questions to understand the history of your relationship and how it developed over time to where it is today. How did you two meet? Was it love at first sight or a friendship that developed as a slow-burn romance? Who asked who out? Where did you go on your first date? How did things progress from there? When did you first move in together? Did one of you propose to the other? Where was your wedding? Who attended?

Was there a reception afterward? These topics are classic fodder for your immigration interview.

Biographic Information

Officers also want you to be familiar with the basic biographical information about your spouse. What is their birthdate? Where were they born? How many siblings do they have? What are their names, and where do they live now? Do they have nieces and nephews? Have they ever been arrested?

For the immigrant spouse, what is their visa immigration history? If either of you have previously been married, why did the prior marriage not work out? If you are the kind of couple who prefers to leave the past in the past, now is a critical time for you to discuss any things you may not have discussed before to ensure you're prepared to answer questions.

Plans for the Future

Officers may also ask about your plans for the future. Are you planning to stay in the area where you live now? Do you want to have children? Are you going to adopt pets? Do you have any vacations planned? Are either of you going back to school soon?

Relationship with Friends & Family

Officers want to understand how you have integrated each other into important aspects of your lives. Have you met each other's family members? Why or why not? Have you attended family celebrations or reunions together? Do you have friends in common? Have you attended work events together?

Travel & Vacations

Officers like to ask about any prior travel or vacations you've taken together. It's a good idea to prepare by reminiscing about various trips you've had so that you will both remember the details if asked about a particular vacation.

Typical questions include: Did you take a train, plane, or drive a car to your destination? Who booked the tickets? Who drove? Did you meet anyone else there? How many days were you gone? If you have any upcoming plans that are already booked, officers would like to hear about that as well.

Celebrations

Every couple is unique in how they celebrate important events and milestones in their relationship. You should be ready to answer questions about any recent religious or cultural holidays you celebrated together, what you did for each other's birthdays and Valentine's Day, and recent gifts you may have given to each other.

Daily Routines

Day-to-day life in marriage is made up of many routines that are unique to each couple. Officers like to ask things like: Who gets up first? What are your work schedules? How is the interior of your house? How do you split up chores? What do you do in your free time together?

Finances

Finances are an important topic of questioning because officers typically believe that financial information is quite personal, and couples who are genuinely in a relationship are likely to know each other's financial situations in great detail. How much does your spouse earn at their job? Are they paid on a weekly or biweekly pay schedule? Is their pay direct deposited or paid by paper check? How much is your monthly rent or mortgage payment? Who is the provider of your electric, cell phones, internet, and utilities? How are your personal bank accounts and joint accounts set up? Do you have life insurance?

The last 24-48 hours

What did you eat for breakfast, lunch, and dinner yesterday? Who cooked? Did you arrive at the interview together or separately? Did you take an Uber, drive yourselves, or walk? Where did you park? When was the last time you saw your stepkids? What time did you go to bed last night? Were you intimate yesterday? No matter what, you need to have a top-of-mind recollection of what you have both been doing over the previous day or two before the interview.

How to Prepare for a Marriage-Based Interview

Obviously, many things that could come up in the interview are things that you will know about your spouse from the time you've already spent together. However, don't underestimate the power of nerves and being in a government office to throw you off a bit, so it's important to be prepared ahead of time even though your relationship is 100% legitimate.

Some people are more or less inclined to remember and retain details about the past, so if you are more forgetful, it's important to review the main topics described above. Plus, it is much easier to recall what you did last Christmas and what you gave each other for Valentine's Day in the comfort of your living room over a glass of wine rather than under the glare of electric lights and an officer's questioning gaze.

Although there are lists of potential marriage immigration interview questions online, take those with a grain of salt. I have seen some fairly aggressive questions online that I have never seen an officer ask in real life. This may be because officers behave better when an attorney is present, or perhaps some of those lists are sensationalized.

Either way, you have nothing to lose—and, in fact, you could make a fun date night out of getting to know each other even a little bit better to make sure that you're thoroughly prepared for your marriage immigration interview!

CHAPTER 9

PLEASE FORGIVE ME! (WAIVERS)

In an ideal world, life would go smoothly, and you would never make any mistakes. However, sometimes life is more complicated than that. Your past experiences or current immigration status could hinder getting a green card through your marriage. Fortunately, in some cases, we can apply for a waiver to seek forgiveness for past mistakes so that we can continue successfully with an immigration case.

The Concept of "Admissibility"

"Admissibility" and "inadmissibility" are important legal terms in U.S. immigration laws. The laws list many possible issues that a potential immigrant could have that make them inadmissible, meaning they are not eligible to get a green card.

This list includes having an unlawful presence in the United States, prior deportations, criminal history, having misrepresented or lied about something previously to the government, and many other things. One of the important jobs of an immigration attorney is to carefully screen clients for any possibility that they could be accused of being inadmissible, and if so, figure out if there is a way to overcome the issue.

Penalties, Exceptions, and Waivers

There is a stated penalty for each ground of inadmissibility that exists in the laws. For some grounds, the inadmissibility automatically ends after a certain amount of time passes. Other grounds have certain exceptions that could be relevant to your situation. And yet other grounds have penalties that remain for a lifetime.

Some of these penalties also have the possibility of a waiver. A waiver is an application that allows you to show the facts of what happened and why you believe you deserve to be legally forgiven for whatever the issue is.

Legal practice in waivers can be extremely complicated because the standards for different waivers are different, the procedures are very complex, and each applicant needs a different customized argument for why they deserve a waiver.

However, it's important to understand that waivers do exist and that immigration attorneys who frequently work with waivers have a very high success rate in obtaining such waivers. Yes, it costs more time, energy, and money to go through the waiver process than if you did not have any grounds of inadmissibility, but sometimes a waiver is the key to solving your immigration problems once and for all and successfully receiving a green card based on your marriage.

If you believe you have any potential complications in your history or current situation, it is very important to get personalized legal advice from an immigration attorney about how these situations impact your immigration options and how best to address these challenges.

CHAPTER 10

REMOVAL OF CONDITIONS

After you successfully receive your green card, it seems fair that you should be done with all the paperwork forever, right?!

Unfortunately, though, that is not the case for many couples. If you have been married for less than two years when you receive your green card, you will need to go through another process later called removal of conditions. In this chapter, we'll talk about what you can expect from the removal of conditions process.

What is removal of conditions?

For couples who have been married for fewer than two years when the green card is received, the type of green card issued is a "conditional" green card. In general, conditional green cards give you the same rights and responsibilities as any other lawful permanent resident.

However, conditional cards are only valid for two years rather than the usual 10 years. Also, conditional green cards include a requirement that you apply to "remove the conditions" before the expiration of the two-year validity period.

What do you have to do to remove the conditions?

To remove the conditions on your residence, you need to send in a specific immigration application requesting to remove the conditions. It must be sent to USCIS within the 90-day period before your conditional green card expires.

In addition to the usual immigration forms and government filing fee, you must also send evidence of your ongoing marriage relationship from when you originally applied for the green card to the present day.

Both spouses are required to participate in signing the forms and submitting evidence to confirm that the marriage relationship has continued and they are still together. This process is required because Congress wanted an anti-fraud measure that ensured people weren't simply getting married for convenience, applying for a green card, and then walking away from the marriage immediately afterward. That is why they check for evidence that your relationship has continued in the two years AFTER receiving the green card.

What if a couple is no longer married or together when it's time to remove the conditions?

It is unfortunate, but there are some situations in which a couple's relationship simply does not last for the two years after receiving a green card. There are some tragic cases where the U.S. citizen petitioner dies, or the couple realizes that they are not compatible and decides to separate or divorce. There are also situations in which the immigrant is a victim of domestic violence and decides to leave the relationship for safety reasons.

Although the system is designed to ensure that people attempting fake marriages will not be able to renew their green cards, fortunately, it does consider that some marriages will not last. The immigrant does not deserve to lose their green card simply because the relationship ultimately did not work out.

There are several situations in which the immigrant spouse can apply for the removal of conditions without the participation of their spouse or former spouse. There is a way to request a special waiver to remove their conditions. Here are the legal bases for the different types of waivers that are available:

- Death of the U.S. petitioner
- Divorce of the couple after they married in good faith
- Immigrant has been abused by the U.S. petitioner after they married in good faith
- Immigrant would suffer hardship if they had to return to their home country

And yes, it is possible to apply on more than one basis. For example, if the immigrant gets divorced because they have been abused and would suffer hardship if they had to return to their home country, we will apply on all three of these bases.

What is the application process like for the removal of conditions?

After you send in the removal of conditions application, fee, and documents, USCIS sends a notice of receipt. This receipt is different from other receipt notices you received earlier in your immigration journey because this receipt also serves as formal proof of an automatic extension of your lawful permanent resident status.

For the length of the extension period, you can show your expired green card, passport, and the extension notice as evidence that you continue to be a lawful permanent resident.

Next, you will either receive a biometrics notice or a notice from USCIS stating that they will be able to reuse your fingerprints that are already on file rather than having you come into the office for new biometrics.

After waiting for some time, you will either receive a final decision or a notice to come in for an in-person interview at a USCIS field office. It is rare for couples to be interviewed when they're applying for removal of conditions together. However, a certain number of cases are selected randomly for interviews, so it's possible!

On the other hand, if you are not applying with your spouse and apply for one of the waivers, you will almost certainly be interviewed in person about the basis for your waiver request.

Once USCIS is satisfied and your case is approved, you will receive a new green card valid for 10 years. Congratulations, you are now an unconditional lawful permanent resident! You can renew your green card every 10 years indefinitely if you wish, or you could decide to apply for U.S. citizenship through naturalization once you are eligible. There's much more information on the naturalization process in the next chapter!

To further simplify your removal of conditions journey, download our free comprehensive chart that breaks down the process step by step. This helpful resource provides a clear overview of each stage, ensuring you have all the information you need. Visit **immigrationforcouples.com/book-vip** to access your free downloadable chart and take the next step toward a successful application!

CHAPTER 11

NATURALIZATION— THE FINISH LINE

Many immigrants' ultimate goal is to become U.S. citizens. This chapter will discuss the process of naturalization, which involves going from being a lawful permanent resident with a green card to becoming a U.S. citizen.

However, the decision about whether or not to naturalize or simply remain a green card holder is very personal. You may remain a green card holder for as long as you wish rather than move forward with U.S. citizenship.

What are the benefits of naturalization?

Naturalization gives immigrants the same legal status as people born in the United States. Once they have lawfully obtained U.S. citizenship through naturalization, it cannot be taken away unless there was fraud in the immigration process.

One of the most important benefits of naturalization is simply the long-term stability it provides. If you are married to a U.S. citizen and have U.S. citizen children also, you may want to become a U.S. citizen to ensure that nothing could happen in politics or your personal situation to cause you to lose your green card.

Every year, a number of green card holders lose their legal status for various reasons and are either deported from the United States or unable to return after absences from the United States. Naturalization can ensure that you will never be one of these people.

U.S. citizenship also provides benefits such as the ability to vote in U.S. elections and to hold certain government jobs. It may even provide certain tax benefits related to inheritance taxes upon your spouse's death.

In addition, once you become a U.S. citizen, you no longer have any of the restrictions you had to live with as a lawful permanent resident. For example, lawful permanent residents must remain physically in the United States for more than half of every year or seek a special permit to be abroad longer. Otherwise, they risk losing their green cards for "abandonment."

Once you are a U.S. citizen, you can stay out of the country for many years and always be able to return without restrictions. You are also no longer required to update your address with the U.S. government or reapply every 10 years and pay the filing fees to renew your green card.

Some green card holders also want to have the opportunity to apply for green cards for their parents, which is not possible as a lawful permanent resident. However, once they become naturalized U.S. citizens, they can submit family-based petitions for their parents or siblings abroad. For many immigrants, these benefits are highly prized, and becoming a U.S. citizen is the natural final step in their immigration journey.

Why do some immigrants not want to naturalize?

There can be a few drawbacks related to becoming a naturalized U.S. citizen for some immigrants. If your original country of citizenship does not permit dual citizenship, then becoming a U.S. citizen means losing your passport and citizenship recognition from your country of origin.

As you decide whether to naturalize, it is important to research whether or not your home country will revoke your citizenship if you naturalize in the United States. Some immigrants choose not to naturalize because they do not plan to stay in the United States forever.

Others simply do not want to be subject to the tax system after they depart the U.S. permanently someday; U.S. citizens must file a tax return annually with the U.S. government, even if they reside abroad.

Still, others may feel they would lose an important part of their identity by becoming a U.S. citizen. The decision of whether or not to apply for naturalization is a very personal one that you can make for yourself.

Who is eligible to apply for naturalization?

If you are married to a U.S. citizen, your earliest opportunity to become a U.S. citizen is three years after you are granted your first green card. If your first green card was a conditional two-year green card, this time still counts toward your three-year total.

Interestingly enough, you don't need to wait until you have been a lawful permanent resident for the entire three years. You can submit your application up to 90 days before the three-year anniversary! Eager applicants will sometimes have me calculate the exact first day they can send their naturalization application—approximately two years and nine months after the date their first card was granted.

Additional requirements include:

- You must be at least 18 years old.

- You must have spent more than half of the past three years physically in the United States (or five years if you aren't married to a U.S. citizen).

- You cannot take trips outside the U.S. for more than one year (and all trips under six months are ideal).

- You must take a test on history and civics in the United States.

- You have to speak, read, and write basic English.

- You must have "good moral character."

What is the process like for naturalization?

Naturalization begins with filing an application along with a filing fee and evidence that you are eligible to become a U.S. citizen. (Yes, you should be used to this by now!) Immigration will then send you either a biometrics notice or a letter stating that they can reuse your fingerprints already on file without having to come to their office for a biometrics appointment again.

At this point, it's good to begin practicing and studying the materials for the naturalization exam!

Eventually, you will receive an appointment for a naturalization interview. At this interview at your local USCIS Field Office, an officer will review your application with you and give you the civics, history, and English tests.

Once USCIS is satisfied that your case is eligible, they will schedule you for an oath ceremony. The oath ceremony is where you formally become a U.S. citizen. Once it's official, you also need to take care of updating your important paperwork, including:

- Applying for a U.S. passport
- Registering to vote
- Notifying the Social Security Administration that you have become a U.S. citizen
- Updating your paperwork with your employer
- Updating paperwork if you changed your name
- Consider petitioning for relatives

And once you've come this far, be sure to do something to celebrate this milestone on your immigration journey. You have come a long way since you began!

To further simplify your naturalization journey, download our free comprehensive chart that breaks down the process step by step. This helpful resource provides a clear overview of each stage, ensuring you have all the information you need. Visit **immigrationforcouples.com/book-vip** to access your free downloadable chart and take the next step toward a successful application!

CHAPTER 12

FINDING JOY IN THE JOURNEY

Throughout our time together, I've discussed the more techni-
cal aspects of the immigration journey. Of course, those aspects
are critically important! However, other, more personal aspects
of the immigration journey for couples are sometimes ignored
completely, to the couple's detriment.

I believe that each couple going through the immigration process
has a unique opportunity to use the challenges of the process to
help fortify the foundation of their relationship rather than allow
the stressors to tear them apart. Being intentional about your
approach to the process can make a world of difference in your
outcome!

The Third Wheel

I've noticed that many couples in the midst of the immigration
process can begin to feel like immigration becomes a "third
wheel" in the relationship. Rather than relating to each other
directly and placing priority on the relationship, it is easy to fall

into the trap of making every conversation between you about the immigration case.

You can choose NOT to make your immigration journey the cornerstone of your relationship. Don't make every personal decision based on your immigration case either. Give the immigration process the attention it deserves, then set it aside!

Managing Stress

Various factors in the immigration process can cause considerable stress, including long wait times, being physically separated, and general uncertainty about the process.

Before starting their immigration case, I recommend that couples seriously contemplate how each tends to respond to stressful situations and make a plan for managing stress. The last thing you want to do is inadvertently blow up at your partner, friends, family, or legal team simply out of frustration with immigration stressors. Regularly managing stress through your preferred methods, be it meditation, taking a walk, or other self-care practices, can keep you healthy and calm throughout the journey.

Stress Is a Choice

Although I've mentioned some potentially stressful factors inherent in the immigration process, I also think it is important to realize that, ultimately, stress is a choice.

If this is the first time you've heard this concept, it might sound surprising. Our society tends to promote the idea that we are all stressed out due to external factors outside our control. External factors indeed impact our lives, but how we respond and manage ourselves is a choice.

You can choose to respond to the immigration process by obsessing over it daily, making it much bigger in your head, and constantly talking to everyone around you about how stressed you are, or you can choose not to let it impact you so much and take steps to manage any stress that arises.

The Immigration Process Can Be Good for Your Relationship

I'd like to take this concept even further and suggest something that may not have occurred to you but that I've seen happen time and time again—the immigration process can be good for your relationship!

How could that be? Here are some of the main ways this happens:

Important Conversations Are Accelerated

The invasive nature of the immigration process requires couples to disclose extensive personal information, prompting discussions on significant topics like finances, religion, and family planning.

These discussions, while perhaps accelerated by the immigration requirements, lead to deeper understanding and alignment between partners. They ensure that couples are not only prepared with evidence for their applications but also in sync with each other's values and life goals.

You Build Resilience and Strength

The immigration journey tests a couple's resolve and union. I speak from personal experience, having gone through the immigration process with my husband. We grew closer together and our resiliency increased for the inevitable challenges life brings.

When you go through hard things, you learn how strong you are. I remember the difficulty of the time my husband and I spent apart during the immigration process, the fear of the unknown, and just wanting to be at the finish line and get out of the feeling of limbo. However, through all those feelings, life still happened, and we made memories and found happiness throughout the process. I see the immigration process now as a parallel to life itself.

You Prepare for Future Life Events

The immigration process also prepares couples for other significant life events that require meticulous documentation and organization. From purchasing a home to applying for graduate programs, the skills honed during the immigration process are transferable and beneficial for future endeavors. It instills discipline and attention to detail, which are invaluable in various aspects of life.

Finding Joy In the Journey

The journey through immigration is often marked by a spectrum of emotions, from anticipation and hope to stress and uncertainty. However, amidst the complexities of paperwork and waiting periods, a profound opportunity exists for personal growth and happiness. You can transform a challenging experience into a period of positive emotional and relational growth.

One key to finding happiness in the immigration process is learning to be present in the moment. Often, our thoughts drift to past experiences or future worries, especially during uncertain times like immigration. By practicing mindfulness and being present, couples can appreciate the current moments in their journey, finding joy in the small, everyday experiences. Techniques like meditation or simple breathing exercises can be instrumental in centering oneself in the present.

Despite the inevitable challenges, the immigration journey can be a time of joy and happiness. Couples can find contentment in working toward a common goal and knowing that each step brings them closer to their dream.

Celebrating small victories, focusing on the love that brought them together, and looking forward to the future can turn the immigration process into a fulfilling and enriching experience. By staying present, practicing gratitude, and supporting each other, couples can transform their immigration experience into a source of joy and happiness.

I hope you find much joy in your immigration journey! Best of luck to you.

CHAPTER 13

WORDS OF WISDOM FROM EXPERIENCED COUPLES

After helping thousands of clients through the U.S. immigration process, I know that sometimes this journey can be challenging. From my experience, I know that even in the toughest moments along the way, you will reach the end and have your happily ever after.

But I know that sometimes it may be hard to see that ending when you are right in the thick of things. That's why I asked several couples who have been through the immigration process what advice and encouragement they would give other couples just starting.

Here is what they had to say:

"Navigating the immigration process can feel overwhelming at times, especially when progress seems slow. However, trusting the process and seeking professional guidance can truly make all the difference.

We've heard stories of people trying to tackle it alone, and it's clear how much unnecessary stress that can bring. For us, it's been a long journey spanning several years, but we are incredibly grateful for Megan and her amazing team.

Without their support, this could have been an incredibly stressful experience. Thanks to their expertise and guidance, the process became a part of our story rather than the focus of our lives.

Now, as we celebrate almost four wonderful years of marriage, we're so thankful that this journey hasn't defined us. Megan's team has been instrumental in making it all feel smooth, and we couldn't recommend them more highly."

–Andres & Crystal Duque

"As we embarked on this journey that we knew was going to be difficult, time-consuming, and emotionally draining, we grounded in our minds that love is a living thing. It needs to be nurtured, cherished, and allowed to grow. Like a garden, our relationship requires attention, care, and constant tending. We had sunny days filled with laughter and joy on the phone, and we also experienced storms that threatened to dampen our spirits. But through it all, we remembered to hold onto each other tightly and remember WHY we were doing this.

Our key was communication. Be open, honest, and kind with your words. Listen with your heart, not just your ears. Seek to understand, not just to be understood, especially since you both are coming from different cultures. Never lose sight of the spark that brought you together. Keep that flame alive through shared passions, intimate moments, difficult conversations, and simple acts of love.

And I will leave you with this: Remember, love is not just a feeling; it's a commitment, a partnership, and a journey you take together. Embrace the adventure, cherish the moments, and build a love that will stand the test of time. May your journey be filled with joy, laughter, and a love that deepens with each passing day, as ours has."

–Carlvin Sylvain Dorvilier & Jessica Dorvilier

"The advice or encouragement we would provide is to be patient in the process. At times, it can be discouraging, but keep a positive attitude and understanding of how immigration works. Keeping your records, pictures, texts, emails, and other supporting documents is crucial.

We went through during COVID and were faced with many delays and long waits. Megan and her team were very supportive and helpful, allowing us to continue our journey with reassurance and confidence that everything would come together. We thank you very much and wish the other couples success in their journey."

–Robert & Michelle Brooke

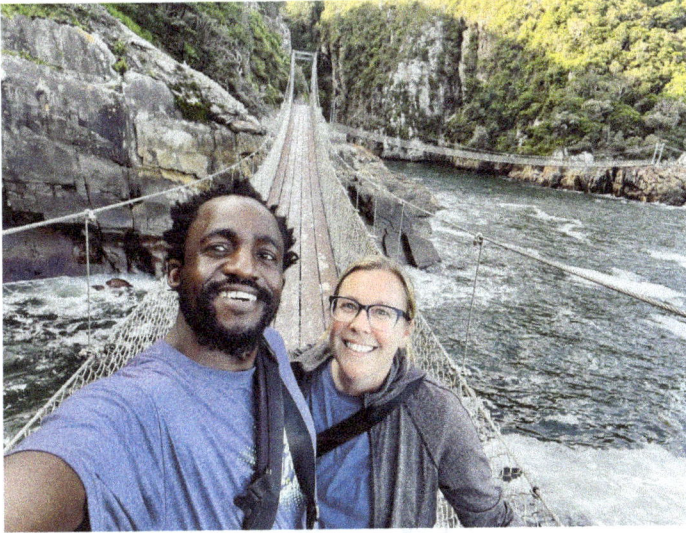

"First of all, you need to keep your eyes on the prize—being together. That's what it's all about.

1. Get Your Paperwork Straight: Make sure you have all your ducks in a row with the paperwork. It's a lot, but ticking things off one at a time can make it feel less overwhelming.

2. Patience is Key: This process isn't a sprint; it's more like one of those long, steady marathons. There will be waits and sometimes no updates for what feels like ages. Just hang tight.

3. Stay Connected: Keep that bond tight while you're sorting out the visa stuff. Video calls, messages, maybe even old-school love letters. Whatever keeps the connection strong. It helps you both feel close and get through the tough parts together.

4. Get Your Information Right: There's tons of info out there, so make sure you're getting your advice from legit sources. Maybe even consider a consultation with an immigration attorney if things look like a tangled mess. That's why we chose Immigration for Couples attorneys. These folks specialize in this area, so they know every detail and rule. From experience, wrong information can waste money and nearly mess up your process. Trust me, Immigration for Couples is the key to your dream.

5. Find Friends Who Get It: Talk to people who have done this before or are doing it now. They can give you tips and make you feel better.

6. Be Prepared for Bumps: Not gonna sugarcoat it—there might be some bumps along the way. Just tackle them one at a time. You got this. Sometimes, things take longer than you hope. Try to be patient and not get too stressed.

7. Keep Your Spirits Up: Throw in some humor, share your dreams, and plan for the future. It's the fuel that'll keep you going. Like my wife and I, we have always shared our dream of buying our beautiful house together, and it happened!

8. Think About the Happy Ending: Remember, you're doing all this to be together. Imagine all the good times ahead. Hang in there! It's a long process, but it's all for a great reason—being together. It's a journey for sure, but at the end of the road, you have a whole new life waiting. Cheers to that!"

–Danmore & Sarah Kusaya

"Starting an immigration journey as a couple can be a deeply emotional and challenging experience. It's a path filled with hope, love, and commitment but also moments of stress, uncertainty, and waiting. From our own experience, here's what we've learned and what we'd like to share with you.

When Kelley and I were going through this process, staying connected was our lifeline. We made it a priority to communicate every single day, whether it was through FaceTime, WhatsApp, or even just a quick text. Those little moments of connection kept us grounded and reminded us that we were in this together. Visiting each other whenever we could was another huge boost for us. Those trips gave us something to look forward to and helped us recharge emotionally. Even though it wasn't always easy to plan, every visit was worth it to keep our relationship strong.

We've also learned how important it is to lean on friends and family. Sharing our journey with them made us feel less alone, and their encouragement helped us stay positive during the tougher moments. At the same time, finding a community of people who were going through similar experiences made a huge difference. We joined social media and WhatsApp groups filled with couples in similar situations. It was comforting to share stories, tips, and even frustrations with people who truly understood what we were experiencing.

During the waiting periods, Kelley and I spent a lot of time talking about our future—our plans, trips we'd take, and adventures we'd go on. Focusing on what was ahead kept us excited and hopeful, even on days when the process felt overwhelming. One thing that really helped us stay connected was our habit of checking in with each other regularly and asking, "What's your percentage today? Are you at 80%, 75%?" If one of us was feeling low, we'd ask, "What can I do to bring you up to 90%? What do you need from me?" Those conversations made us feel supported and reminded us that we were truly in this together.

The paperwork and legal processes can feel daunting, and we're so glad we reached out to Immigration for Couples when we needed guidance. Having an experienced immigration lawyer helped us navigate everything more smoothly and allowed us to focus on supporting each other. Of course, we had moments of doubt and frustration, but we always tried to lift each other up. Reminding ourselves of why we started this journey and how much we wanted to be together kept us motivated. Encouraging each other made all the difference.

The stress of immigration can be overwhelming at times. We made it a point to check in regularly and talk about how we were feeling. If you're struggling, don't hesitate to seek support from a counselor or therapist. Your mental health is just as important as the process itself.

Starting an immigration journey isn't easy, but we've found that love, determination, and the right support can get you through it. Every step you take brings you closer to the life you're building together, so that long journey is well worth it in the end."

–Denis Garneau & Kelley McClain-Garneau

"Our advice would be to find something to do together that you can make some sort of progress in. For example, play an online game, start a TV series together, make a craft, etc. You're not always going to have an interesting day to talk about, and doing something together other than talking eases the pressure of keeping the conversation going.

Also, don't be afraid of silence; not every second needs to be filled with words. When we focus on constantly filling time with conversation, it dilutes the meaningful things we have to say."

–Bowen & Cassandra Brooks

"First and foremost, focus on each other and continue to strengthen your relationship. Spend time during the long wait to plan for your future together.

Secondly, educate yourselves on the immigration process. There are lots of good sources on the internet that can help you antici-pate the next steps and ensure that you are doing everything pos-sible to help Megan's team put forth the strongest case.

And lastly, keep living your lives. We were lucky in the sense that we were together throughout the process. We stayed very active, especially spending time outdoors (hiking) and with family and friends, which ultimately helped to manage the inevitable stress and to pass the time more quickly."

–Dan Collishaw & Beth Porteza

"Our best advice would be to be organized and stay focused. Don't wait to start or for the perfect time because the sooner everything is submitted, the earlier you'll hear back. Also, make sure all the documents are signed. Finding evidence for "proof of relationship" may seem strange and overwhelming, but if you are true to the process, things will go smoothly.

Focus on the relationship; it's the most important aspect of the entire process. This process can be consuming and emotionally draining, so you must find time for each other, whether it be video/phone calls, messages, emails, letters, etc.

Here are some other words of advice from us:

- Be patient.
- Find the positive in the wait.
- Don't be afraid to ask questions or to ask for help."

–Stephan Jones & Karol Zuniga

"Keep any and all supporting documents you have. Even the littlest things add up. It's much better to provide more than they need than to provide less. Also, be honest about everything up front because everything is a lot smoother if you tell the truth the whole time."

–Dakotah & Thao Wealing

"Be patient, get organized, and follow Megan's instructions. She and her staff helped us navigate this process at the end of the first Trump administration and the start of the global pandemic. It was not an ideal situation, but Megan and her team made us feel like we were all on a team together. Don't forget that you are part of a team and that you all have the same goal during the process.

1. One step at a time. The process may feel daunting, long, and insurmountable, but by taking one step at a time, it becomes manageable and not so nerve-wracking.

2. It's just about a document; it's not about your love or connection. Even if things don't work out, you can find a different place to settle in.

3. The interview itself was a piece of cake. I was so stressed about it. No one wanted to stop us from being together; it was just a bureaucratic procedure without evil intent.

4. There is no reason to panic; every challenge has several solutions. No one has their documents perfectly organized and gathered over time; some things are easily accessed, others are not. This is part of the process.

5. Take care of yourselves, practice self-care; it's not worth it to waste your mental and physical health on this."

–Chris & Anastasia Ekman

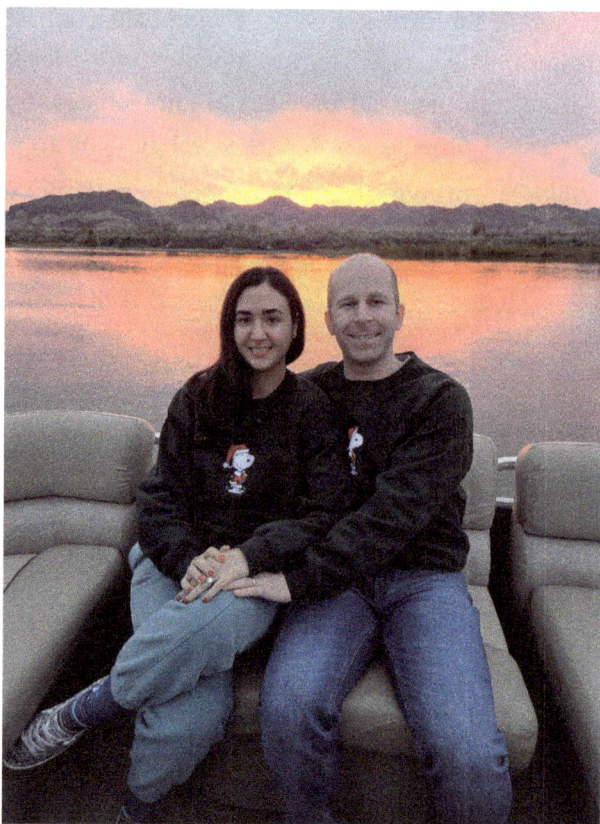

"There are certain things that you can't control. They will remain out of your control whether or not you choose to worry about them.

- Your immigration journey will not go to plan. You will have at least one setback or delay. Don't get discouraged by this.

- Your immigration journey will be more expensive than you expect. There are far more costs than just the governmental fees. Don't be surprised when you realize this.

- It can be helpful to consult trusted groups that share reliable info, but in general, don't listen to people on social media. If you want to find something out, do your own research. The information and resources are out there.

Consult an immigration attorney before beginning your immigration journey. Not necessarily hire, but at least consult. You don't know what you don't know.

It boils down to not worrying about what you can't control, expect the unexpected, and keep yourself informed with reliable info."

–Daniel Tiano & Ana Rodriguez Humpierre

"The decision to get the K-1 visa was a challenge; you need to have love, patience, and perseverance, among other things. This path is really challenging and demanding; just stay calm and know yourself well so everything will be a little easier for you. After many difficult moments, we are now planning our wedding and enjoying life together in the United States. Good luck!"

–Tony LaRosa &
Learikaren Amundarain Ospina

"It may not feel like it right now, but it really is just a matter of time before you're together again. No matter how long, frustrating, and stressful the journey may be—if the love is real, you are going to get there. Two and a half years into the process, with two kids and about a dozen plane tickets to show for it, we are finally all together. It's the best feeling in the world. I promise it's all worth it."

–Abdiqani Jamal Abdirahman
& Madilyn Smith

CLOSING

As we conclude this book, I want to take a moment to reflect on the incredible journey you are embarking on as a couple navigating the U.S. marriage immigration process.

Throughout these chapters, we have explored the various paths available to you, examined the steps involved, and addressed the hurdles that may arise. I hope to empower you with the knowledge and tools to turn what can feel like an overwhelming experience into a manageable and joyful journey.

The immigration process is undoubtedly a complex web of legal requirements, paperwork, and emotional challenges. However, I want to remind you that at the heart of this journey is love—your love for each other and your dream of a shared future.

Every step you take together, whether gathering documentation, preparing for interviews, or simply discussing your next steps, brings you closer to your goal of building a life together in the United States. Remember, it's okay to feel apprehensive, but don't allow fear to hold you back. Instead, embrace the knowledge you've gained from this book and utilize it as a stepping stone to take swift and informed action.

Reflect on the importance of the decisions that lie ahead. Each choice you make is a testament to your commitment to one another and your shared dreams. Whether it's selecting the right immigration path, gathering evidence to demonstrate your relationship, or preparing for the marriage interview—these moments are vital opportunities for growth and strengthening your bond. Many couples have successfully navigated this path before you, and their experiences serve as powerful reminders that perseverance, preparation, and partnership can lead to triumph.

As you close this book and perhaps take a moment to gather your thoughts, I encourage you to consider the next steps. Whether you feel compelled to reach out to an experienced immigration attorney, dive deeper into specific chapters that resonate with your situation, or simply discuss your insights and plans with your partner, take action! The journey to securing your future together begins with the decision to move forward, even if the path appears challenging.

Ultimately, remember that each of you possesses the power to shape your story. Trust in your decisions, embrace the process, and, most importantly, support one another as you navigate the twists and turns ahead. The immigration journey is about more than just paperwork; it's about love, commitment, and the incredible potential you hold as a couple to overcome obstacles and create a fulfilling life together.

Now is your time to take the reins of your journey. With the right mindset and a commitment to action, you can transform your dreams into reality. Go forth with courage, confidence, and clarity—your adventure is just beginning!

NEXT STEPS

Thank you for embarking on this journey with me! I invite you to continue exploring the U.S. marriage immigration process by visiting our website at **immigrationforcouples.com**. Sign up for our newsletter to receive valuable insights, updates, and resources straight to your inbox.

Do you want to ask me your questions live? I host a weekly live immigration attorney chat on Facebook, YouTube, LinkedIn, and Instagram, where I share tips, answer questions, and provide support to couples navigating their immigration journeys. Please follow my firm's social media channels so you can join me for the next live-stream event.

If you're ready to take the next step, I encourage you to schedule a consultation through our website. Together, we can create a personalized plan that meets your needs and helps you achieve your immigration goals.

Your journey matters, and I am here to help you every step of the way. If you found this book helpful, please consider leaving a review on Amazon—your feedback not only helps us improve but also supports other couples needing guidance. Let's continue to build a community of love, support, and successful journeys!

Ways to Stay Connected

Website: immigrationforcouples.com
YouTube Channel: youtube.com/@immigrationforcouples7362
Facebook: facebook.com/immigrationforcouples
Instagram: instagram.com/immigrationforcouples
LinkedIn: linkedin.com/company/immigration-for-couples
Podcast: immigrationforcouples.com/podcast/

Throughout this book, I have included a link to downloadable resources to guide you on your journey. I'm also including a scannable QR code to easily access those resources.

immigrationforcouples.com/book-vip

ACKNOWLEDGMENTS

I want to express my deepest gratitude to my husband, my unwavering supporter and greatest cheerleader. Our own immigration journey, filled with twists, turns, and challenging moments, has not only shaped our lives but has also inspired me to become an immigration attorney and guide for couples navigating the U.S. immigration process. Thank you for believing in my dreams—from law school to writing this book—and for reminding me that we are always stronger together. Our journey is a beautiful testament to resilience, and I am eternally grateful for your love, support, and partnership in every step we take.

I wish to extend my heartfelt appreciation to my firm administrator, Julie, whose invaluable support and dedication have been instrumental in bringing this book to life. Through countless planning sessions, brainstorming meetings, and meticulous reviews, you have helped transform my vision into reality. Your keen insights, organizational skills, and encouragement have been a guiding force throughout this journey. Thank you for your unwavering commitment and for being such an essential part of this endeavor; I truly could not have done it without you.

I am sincerely grateful to the hundreds of couples I have had the privilege to represent and serve. Thank you for trusting my team and me to guide you on your immigration journey and for sharing your personal stories and experiences with such openness and vulnerability. Your resilience and determination in facing challenges have deeply inspired me and shaped my passion for this work. Your journeys motivated me to write this book to empower other couples as they navigate the complexities of the U.S. immigration process. Together, we forge a path of hope and success, and I am honored to be part of your stories.

Lastly, I want to acknowledge my incredible team at Immigration for Couples. Each of you plays a vital role in representing the couples we serve, bringing your unique strengths and areas of expertise to the forefront. Together, we have earned the trust of our clients during one of the most pivotal times in their lives, and our collective efforts have resulted in outcomes that truly change lives. I am deeply grateful for your dedication, collaboration, and passion for our mission. It is a joy to work alongside each of you as we make a meaningful impact together.

ABOUT THE AUTHOR

Megan Pastrana is the CEO and Managing Attorney of Immigration for Couples. She and her team are dedicated to holistically assisting couples to navigate the U.S. immigration process to start the next chapter of their lives together.

Megan serves her clients not only as an immigration attorney but also as a mindset coach and guide throughout the immigration process. Having experienced her own journey of love and immigration with her husband, she understands firsthand the emotions and difficulties that couples experience. In fact, her decision to found Immigration for Couples resulted from her personal immigration journey with her husband.

She believes it is her calling to help couples navigate the ever-evolving and complex labyrinth of immigration. Megan strives to empower couples to view the immigration process as an uplifting experience and an opportunity to grow and strengthen their relationship.

The immigration process is long and has many twists and turns. Throughout the case, she helps couples focus on their relationship and the aspects of the case that they can control instead of allowing stress and frustration to consume them.

Megan also hosts the podcast *Navigating Love & Immigration.* Additionally, she has provided her immigration policy expertise to members of Congress, reality TV show producers, and several major media outlets, including *Telemundo, LA Weekly, Maxim,* and ABC. She has been recognized as one of the top immigration attorneys in the nation by *Super Lawyers.*

In her free time, she enjoys spending time on her family's farm, going on walks with her dogs, and traveling the world with her husband. They have visited Mexico, the United Arab Emirates, China, Costa Rica, Scotland, and Italy, among other places.

www.ingramcontent.com/pod-product-compliance
Lightning Source LLC
Chambersburg PA
CBHW071431210326
41597CB00020B/3750